UNQUIET TIME.

a devotional for the rest of us

BY
Heather Caliri

Praise

"Many of us come to the Bible carrying the weight of expectation, fear, or inner baggage, longing for the Bible to become more than the book we study in order to perform. What if it becomes a story we enter, one that opens our hearts to a mysterious God? In Unquiet Time Heather Caliri gives us the tools to explore our questions, and follow them all the way into God's loving presence. It is an approachable, interactive, challenging, and beautiful book."

-Micha Boyett, author of Found:
A Story of Questions, Grace, & Everyday Prayer

"In Unquiet Time, Heather Caliri bravely and boldly invites you to a journey of discovery and transformation. The often surprising, sometimes wonderfully disruptive exercises will stretch you, nourish you, and call you to a deeper, truer love for the God who longs to be known by you.

-Jerusha Clark, author of
Every Thought Captive and The Life You Crave

"As disarming as it is invitational, <u>Unquiet Time</u> deftly moves past our tired defenses to reopen our hearts to the Bible. This is a book that artfully takes our heart's pulse, even as it nudges us to ask: "How would I read the Bible if I was not afraid?"

-Suzanne Burden, co-author of
<u>Reclaiming Eve</u>

ACKNOWLEDGEMENTS

keri Smith, whose books, Wreck this Journal and How to be an Explorer of the World, inspired this project.

☆

Joy McCullough Carranza, whose chutzpah in faith, life & art helps me see what 'keeping the faith' means.

☆

My daughters, Julia & Lucy, who always teach me how to pay attention.

☆

My husband, Dyami, who reminded me to exhale.

INSTRUCTIONS

1. There is no right way. Follow the living fire of the SPIRIT, not the directions.

2. Take a deep breath. Don't forget to exhale.

3. Be kind to yourself. You are God's beloved child.

4. When possible, get your body involved. Gesture. Speak aloud. Dance your response. Pray in child's pose. Sing a song if it strikes you.

5. Notice your feelings, fears, & what you'd rather not say out loud. Say them out loud.

MORE INSTRUCTIONS

6. God is with you, even if you forget to ask him.

7. Have fun.

8. Go.

~ one last thing : ~

a brave thing also
could be not finishing
this devotional as an act
of worship & faith.
God could complete
it instead of you.
Just sayin'.

"I am going through another period of finding it hard to read the Bible... It would be wrong to get fussed about it. Far better to trust that after wobbling a bit the compass will come to rest in the right direction."

Dietrich Bonhoeffer.

"We tend to read in order to find out something that will work for us..."

M. Robert Mulholland Jr.

WRITE
DOWN ALL
THE RULES
ABOUT
READING
THE
BIBLE.

THE RULES

1.

2.

3.

4.

5.

6.

CONTINUE ON THE NEXT PAGE.

MORE RULES

7.

8.

9.

10.

11.

12.

13.

14.

Sit with God & the rules for a while.
Ask Him whose they are.

"Abbot Lot came to Abbot Joseph and said: Father, according as I am able, I keep my little rule, and my little fast, my prayer, meditation, and contemplative silence... Now, what more shall I do?

The elder rose up in reply and stretched out his hands to heaven, and his fingers became like ten lamps of fire. He said,

WHY NOT BE TOTALLY CHANGED INTO FIRE?"

THE WISDOM OF THE DESERT

Inside the hand, write a list of words describing how you wish you read the Bible.

Now: pray through each word.

Lift each one up to God.

Then be quiet for a while.

DONE?

Leave the list in God's hands.

"We want life to have meaning,

We want fulfillment,
healing,
and even ecstasy,
but the human paradox
is that we
find these things
by starting where
we are, not where
we wish we were."

KATHLEEN NORRIS

What is your least favorite Bible passage? List it here.

Now play art critic: What would you like if you liked it?
OR: where is the justice/freedom in disliking that passage?

SOURCE: <u>Still</u> by Lauren Winner

It is of the very nature of the Bible to affront, perplex & astonish the human mind.

Hence, the reader who opens the Bible must be prepared for disorientation, incomprehension, perhaps outrage. THOMAS MERTON

TELL ME MORE.

"Before familiarity can turn into awareness the familiar must be stripped of its inconspicuousness."

BERTOLT BRECHT

CANON:

a provocation.

Books in various Christian Canons:

Protestant: 66

Catholic: 73

Ethiopian Orthodox: 81

1st

Buy a Bible at the thrift store. Cut the Binding to Separate the books. Channel Martin Luther. What stays in?

Luther wanted to cut Hebrews, James, Jude and Revelation.

2nd

Make two piles. Pray over each, asking God to use, uncover, redeem & challenge you with them.

Source: Steve Chalke, Restoring Confidence in the Bible

The first Christians PRAYED & WORSHIPPED for several generations before they had a WRITTEN CREED and they prayed for several HUNDRED YEARS before they had a canon of Scripture

DIANA BUTLER BASS
CHRISTIANITY AFTER RELIGION

How would you read the Bible if you were not afraid? What would need to change for you to read without fear? How might God bless you through fearlessness?

more on fearlessness: go!

Come, come,
Whoever you are.
Wanderer, worshipper,
lover of leaving.

It doesn't matter.

Ours is not a caravan
of despair.

Come, even if you
have broken your vow
a hundred times.

Come, yet again,
come, come. RUMI

found poetry

Use a Sharpie to cross out words, blocks, phrases. The leftover words are your poem.

even in my temple[z] I find their wickedness,"
    declares the LORD.
12"Therefore their path will become slippery;[a]
they will be banished to darkness and there they will fall.
I will bring disaster on them in the year they are punished,[b]"
    declares the LORD.

13"Among the prophets of Samaria I saw this repulsive thing:
They prophesied by Baal[c] and led my people Israel astray.[d]
14And among the prophets of Jerusalem I have seen something horrible:[e]
They commit adultery and live a lie.[f]
They strengthen the hands of evildoers,[g]
so that no one turns from his wickedness.[h]
They are all like Sodom[i] to me;
the people of Jerusalem are like Gomorrah."[j]

15"Therefore, this is what the LORD Almighty says concerning the prophets:

"I will make them eat bitter food and drink poisoned water,[k]
because from the prophets of Jerusalem

23:11 [z]S 2Ki 21:4;
S Jer 7:10
23:12 [a]S Dt 32:35;
S Job 3:23;
Jer 13:16
[b]Jer 11:23
23:13 [c]S 1Ki 18:22
[d]ver 32;
S Isa 3:12;
Eze 13:10
23:14 [e]S Jer 5:30;
Hos 6:10
[f]Jer 29:23
[g]ver 22
[h]S Isa 5:18
[i]S Ge 18:20;
Mt 11:24
[j]Jer 20:16;
Am 4:11
23:15 [k]S Jer 8:14;
9:15 [l]S Jer 8:10
23:16 [m]Jer 27:9-10,
14; S Mt 7:15
[n]S Jer 14:14;
Eze 13:3
[o]Jer 9:20
23:17 [p]ver 31

[q]S 1Ki 22:8;
S Jer 4:10
[r]S Jer 13:10
[s]Jer 5:12;
Am 9:10;
Mic 3:11
23:18 [t]S 1Ki 22:19;
S Ro 11:34
23:19 [u]Isa 30:30;
Jer 25:32; 30:23
[v]Zec 7:14
23:20

'The LORD says: You will have peace.'[q]
And to all who follow the stubbornness[r] of their hearts
they say, 'No harm[s] will come to you.'
18But which of them has stood in the council[t] of the LORD
to see or to hear his word?
Who has listened and heard his word?
19See, the storm[u] of the LORD will burst out in wrath,
a whirlwind[v] swirling down on the heads of the wicked.
20The anger[w] of the LORD will not turn back[x]
until he fully accomplishes the purposes of his heart.
In days to come you will understand it clearly.
21I did not send[y] these prophets,
yet they have run with their message;
I did not speak to them,
yet they have prophesied.
22But if they had stood in my council,[z]
they would have proclaimed[a] my words to my people
and would have turned[b] them from their evil ways
and from their evil deeds.[c]

"Answers
did not
satisfy
but questions
brought me
low before
God."

K.D. Byers

SURPRISE!

How do you wish the bible would surprise you?

What would surprise look like?

IT IS FINE SOMETIMES TO SIMPLY SAY, "I HAVE NO IDEA" AND "WE REALLY JUST DON'T KNOW."

CHRISTIAN SMITH

Embody

Source:
An altar in
the world
Barbara
Brown Taylor

BEGINNER
ACT OUT A BEATITUDE OR A PARABLE WITH PANTOMIME

ADVANCED
INVITE SOME FRIENDS TO DO IT WITH YOU.

[DO WE] BELEIVE THAT THERE WILL BE NEWNESS [OR] ONLY THAT WILL THERE WILL BE... A MOVING OF THE PIECES INTO NEW PATTERNS? WALTER BRUEGGEMANN

How could
you move
from trying
harder
to opening
your heart?

What Now?

Yearning for more honest questions about the Bible? You're in luck!

Subscribers to my blog will get the director's cut of this book.

Go to heathercaliri.com/directorscut/ to find out more.

Another bonus? You'll score a free copy of my first e-book, "Dancing Back to Jesus: Post-perfectionist faith in five easy verbs."

Sources

Bass, Diana Butler. 2012. Christianity After Religion: The End of Church and the Birth of a New Spiritual Awakening. New York: HarperOne.

Brecht, Bertolt. Quoted in How to Be an Explorer of the World: Portable Life Museum by Keri Smith, 2008. New York: Perigee.

Bonhoeffer, Dietrich. Quoted in Opening the Bible by Thomas Merton, 1972. London: George Allen & Unwin Ltd.

Byers, K.D. 2013. A woman of many questions. In Talking Taboo: American Christian

Women Get Frank About Faith. Ashland, Or: White Cloud Press.

Chalke, Steve. 2014. Restoring Confidence in the Bible. Oasis UK. Kindle ebook.

Merton, Thomas, trans. 1960. The Wisdom of the Desert. New York: New Directions Books.

_____. 1972. Opening the Bible. London: George Allen & Unwin Ltd.

Mulholland, M. Robert Jr. 1985. Shaped by the Word: The Power of Scripture in Spiritual Formation. Nashville: The Upper Room.

Norris, Kathleen. 1998. The Quotidian Mysteries: Laundry, Liturgy, and "Women's Work". New York: Paulist Press.

Rumi. Quoted in *The Artist's Rule: Nurturing Your Creative Soul with Monastic Wisdom* by Christine Valters Paintner. 2011. Notre Dame, Ind.: Sorin Books.

Smith, Christian. 2011. *The Bible Made Impossible: Why Biblicism Is Not a Truly Evangelical Reading of Scripture.* Grand Rapids: Brazos.

Smith, Keri. 2012. *Wreck This Journal (Black) Expanded Ed.* New York: Perigee Trade.

Taylor, Barbara Brown. 2009. *An Altar in the World.* New York: HarperOne.

Winner, Lauren F. 2012. *Still: Notes on a Mid-Faith Crisis.* New York: HarperOne.

Printed in Great Britain
by Amazon